COTSWOLD
STONE BARNS

TIM JORDAN

AMBERLEY

First published 2011

Amberley Publishing
The Hill, Stroud,
Gloucestershire, GL5 4EP

www.amberleybooks.com

Copyright © Tim Jordan, 2011

The right of Tim Jordan to be identified as the
Author of this work has been asserted in accordance
with the Copyrights, Designs and Patents Act 1988.

ISBN 978 1 4456 0181 6

British Library Cataloguing in Publication Data.
A catalogue record for this book is available from
the British Library.

Typeset in 9.5pt on 12pt Celeste.
Typesetting by Amberley Publishing.
Printed in the UK.

INTRODUCTION

Barns have been part of the landscape since the Middle Ages. Their relatively simple architecture provides a window onto a number of aspects of our rural history and traditions, each having their own distinguishing regional characteristics. As such they frequently display a harmony with their surroundings, none more so, I would argue, than in the Cotswolds, where their essential defining characteristics come from the local oolitic limestone. It influences both their appearance and construction and provides some of the most attractive roofing materials to be found anywhere.

A number of superb medieval examples dating from the thirteenth to the fifteenth century can still be found throughout the Cotswolds, though most of the barns in the region today were built between the mid to late 1600s and 1900. They can be seen guarding the farmstead, reflecting the wealth of an estate, providing space for storing grain, sheering sheep or processing feedstuffs, along with the many hundreds of field barns high on a wold or down in a sheltered valley providing cover for hay and shelter to animals as a satellite from the home farm.

Several barns frequently exhibited a number of unusual and indeed unique features which have often been overlooked or ignored especially since the majority of these stone barns are now redundant, incompatible with twenty-first-century machinery and intensive farming. Despite this, and the fact that many have indeed disappeared over recent decades, substantial numbers remain and are increasingly recognised as part of our vernacular and agricultural heritage.

While most features were essentially functional, several have been elaborated on by the craftsmen who took a pride in their construction. Ventilation slits can be found in parts of the Cotswolds which have an added diamond shaped hole above, giving them a 'candle-flame'-like appearance. Owl holes can be seen with an elaborate trefoil entrance or an added convenient perching ledge. Other adornments which *only* appear to serve a decorative function are the many forms of finials, the final embellishment above the gable ends, perhaps signifying a 'job well done'; though several of these earlier ones would seem to have had a religious significance. Apotropaic markings, though not essential to the structural integrity of the building, can frequently be found inscribed on the door jambs or in cart entrances and were believed to ward off evil spirits. Some barns reflect the wealth of the original owners not simply by their size but by the quality of the stonework, elaborate porch entrances or canopies, even fine mullioned windows. Others have quite elaborate carvings embedded in their walls which have served to illustrate their function or purpose; some adornments simply appear to be additions from a previous building but which the owner apparently considered it would be 'a pity to throw away'.

This book aims to provide a pictorial essay from the earliest surviving medieval monastic estate and tithe barns, through some of the substantial barns which were built when the wool trade picked up again in the Cotswolds after the Civil War, the Agricultural Revolution and the advent of increasing mechanisation – so tracing their adaptation and changing functions as farming practices evolved over time – to the period when no further stone barns were built. As such it can be seen as complementary to an earlier book of mine on *Cotswold Barns* (published by Tempus in 2006 and recently reprinted by The History Press) which discusses in more detail the design, construction methods and changing patterns of use of these buildings in the rural economy and environment. This volume also focuses on a number of the Cotswolds' characteristic features which may be unique to an area or craftsman, even to an individual barn. Many of these features may be equally vulnerable to the mini revival of some of these buildings for such alternative uses as community functions, business enterprises and most commonly for conversion to domestic housing.

CONTENTS AND HISTORICAL SUMMARY

COTSWOLDS and the Limestone Belt

10 miles

▲ Selected surviving medieval barns

The Jurassic Limestone belt
(Cotswolds inset)

BARNS IN THE LANDSCAPE

These initial images reflect the range in both size and location of barns across the region. They also serve to illustrate several of the features considered in more detail later. The majority of barns tend to be grouped close to the farmhouse and related buildings, and are usually the most prominent of the farm buildings. This is clearly the case at Frocester Court (below), where in the Middle Ages the practice was to store as much of the grain crops as possible in the barn, only using ricks as a last resort.

ISOLATED FIELD BARNS

It is not uncommon in the Cotswolds to come across small field barns serving land some considerable distance from the home farmstead. These began to appear in the eighteenth century and continued to be built into the nineteenth century. Many had attendant shelter sheds for cattle, with a small enclosed yard, as with Chalkhill Barn (between Turkdean and Notgrove, above), and often with the entrance offset to one side, as with the barn between Windrush and Sherborne (below).

STANWAY AND SOMERFORD KEYNES

Constructed in the warm mellow stone typical of the Guiting area, Stanway, like most villages at the time, had its own quarry – the Jackdaw quarry – and the quarry at Stump Cross a mile or so up the nearby hill. Built in 1370 for the Abbot of Tewkesbury, it reflects the power and dominance of the Church in the Cotswolds during this period. The Manor Barn at Somerford Keynes (1753) provides an excellent indicator of the later shift in power to a more secular clientele of wealthy laymen and merchants.

FARMSTEAD GROUPS

North Cerney Manor Farm has an elegant late eighteenth-century double barn with projecting porches and adjoining stable block and buildings, similarly built of random limestone with dressed quoins under the ubiquitous stone slate roof. Below, sheltered in the valley, is a delightful group of buildings in the hamlet of Duntisbourne Leer, where the stream flows down from the surrounding hillside, passing between the collection of buildings via a ford, before continuing its journey.

SELECTED SURVIVING MEDIEVAL BARNS

Medieval barns varied in size, though it is chiefly the larger ones which have survived. Middle Littleton (above) provides a useful example to begin our look at these buildings. Built in the thirteenth century for Evesham Abbey by Abbot John de Brokehampton, it reflects the wealth and influence of the great lords of church and state.

The drawing below illustrates the essential construction process. Scaffolding was internal, with trestles and platforms supported on poles protruding through the putlog holes in the walls as the building rose.

MIDDLE LITTLETON

The barn has eleven bays: the two end ones are aisled and the remainder are of a raised cruck construction. The unusual double tie beams can be clearly seen, as can a number of other interesting features. Two tiers of arched wind braces are used to prevent the rafters from raking and in the middle right-hand side one can just see the foot of the cruck has been enlarged by a wedge of timber to provide additional strength at that point. The putlog holes are retained for ventilation.

Note: A major incentive for the early building of barns was the tithe, but as we shall see, not all large barns were tithe barns. A tithe (or tenth) of an individual's annual produce was paid to the clergy as an ecclesiastical tax in support of the parish priest or rector, to help with relief for the poor and upkeep of the church. This was stored in a tithe barn, often near the church, hence the tendency to regard any large barn as a tithe barn. In practice many parishes had a rector who was not the parish priest: here the rectorial duties and benefits might be in the hands of a monastery or college – and monastic establishments often had several barns.

SIDDINGTON

This is also partially aisled and of a similar base cruck construction built in the thirteenth century. Although it now has five bays, evidence suggests it was originally longer at its western end. Traces also appear in the fabric indicating subsequent changes which took place when it was converted to a malting; the north porch was enlarged for a kiln, the main barn was lofted throughout (now removed), dormers and an outside staircase were added. Until recently it had been used as a working stable together with an attached eighteenth-century barn and other buildings.

FROCESTER COURT

The estate barn was built by Abbot John de Gamages between 1284 and 1306 and is still a working farm. At 57 metres in length, it is one of the longest in the country (see also p. 6). Between the two wagon porches are three flying buttresses added in the nineteenth century which provide support to the shifting wall. Having been roofed over, these now serve as animal pens with metal doors, though they are difficult to see from any distance today due to modern sheds having been built up close – a feature not unusual with many such barns.

THE GREAT BARN AT COXWELL

This cathedral-like building was a monastic grange built by the Cistercian monks of Beaulieu Abbey. Before dissolution it is estimated that the Cistercians had some 2,000 barns in England, providing an excellent illustration of the wealth and influence such groups held during this period. While urging its flock to seek their riches in heaven, the medieval Church was not averse to stockpiling its riches on earth. Wool, for example, was a highly significant commodity in the Cotswold economy; the Abbot of Gloucester alone owned some 10,000 sheep.

STANWAY AND CHURCH ENSTONE

Built for the Abbot of Tewkesbury, Stanway has changed very little over its 600 years. It too has striking finials above each of the gable ends, which are reminiscent of the ones at Middle Littleton. The manor and parish of Church Enstone had belonged to the Benedictine abbey of Winchcombe since the ninth century, and in 1382 the Abbot erected this barn at the request of the bailiff of the monastic grange at Enstone; the event is noted on the inserted date stone.

BREDON

Built by the Bishop of Worcester in 1344, this barn remained in the hands of the bishops until 1559; hence it was quite separately administered from a nearby rectorial tithe barn. It has two large wagon porches on the north side, one containing lofted accommodation for the granger or reeve – reached, as we see above, by an external staircase. Unusual is the hexagonal chimney with a decorative cowling. Notice that all of these large extended porches have a smaller 'final exit' door to the side!

GRANGER'S ACCOMMODATION AND INTERIOR

The granger's accommodation is furnished with a fireplace and immediately to its left a garderobe – dropping to a pit some 5 metres below. The small door to the rear leads to a gallery overlooking the interior of the barn, allowing the granger to oversee the threshing and winnowing of grain as well as keeping a wary eye out for any pilfering. Though badly damaged by fire in 1980, as can be seen from the charred roofing and aisle timbers below, it has been restored to its imposing original design.

ASHLEWORTH

The entire manor at Ashleworth was given to the abbey at Bristol in the mid-twelfth century and ran as a farming enterprise at Ashleworth Court. The tithe barn itself was built between 1481 and 1515 and is a large ten-bay barn, originally separated internally by a dividing wall. It has two elegant gabled cart entrances with correspondingly smaller exit doors opposite. The roof timbers are an excellent example of queen post trusses, and worth noting too are the ashlar stone buttresses at each corner point of the building.

BRADFORD-ON-AVON

This barn was built in the mid-fourteenth century and served Barton farm, one of the farms of the abbey, which was a Benedictine nunnery. The barn was primarily used as storage for the farm, though it is likely that the parish tithes may also have been stored in it. The magnificent raised cruck roof has trusses of a similar profile as far as the collars, only varying after that point. In contrast to many such barns, the whole of the masonry is of coursed ashlar stone.

ABLINGTON

Post-Dissolution, many monastic estates passed to courtiers and county functionaries, and following the Civil War a century later, when the wool trade again picked up, a number of elegant barns were built. Though not on the same scale of their earlier predecessors, they nevertheless often followed a similar design. Thus, the barn began to slowly reflect development and changes in both social and political power. Ablington Manor's barn has a date stone marked '1727 JC'; John Cowell was lord of the manor at that time.

BARNS NEAR CHERINGTON AND GREAT BARRINGTON

Lowesmoor Farm above is another fine eighteenth-century example, while the Manor Farmhouse at Great Barrington faces a pair of large barns, each of which show late seventeenth-century classical touches but all in Cotswold style. The rounded pitching holes in the gable ends were thought to cause less damage to the sheaves as they were tossed in. As a landscape, the Cotswolds reflect a number of prosperous middle-sized estates; the barn was often a visible expression of the owner's wealth where the quality of stonework or decoration went beyond the basic functional purpose – undoubtedly the case here at Barrington.

COTSWOLD STONE ROOFING

At this point it is worthwhile to consider briefly the nature and characteristics of the ubiquitous stone roofing on these barns. Naturally occurring, the stone was laid down in thin layers (and split either by hand or frost); it was left to the 'slatters' to trim them. Sizes generally varied from 2 feet to 6 inches, and so are graduated from eaves to ridge, many with beautifully swept valleys between barn roof and porch. Something of their 'attractiveness' can be seen on the barn below – the lower courses above the shelter sheds and the porch entrance have been 'removed' and replaced with modern slates and some protective barbed wire!

FIELD BARNS

These began to be built in the eighteenth century, generally to serve outlying land from the main farmstead. Ernest Waller, for example, bought the manor at Turkdean and Hazleton in 1725 and built several barns in the surrounding area – a number of them bearing his initials with a date stone on their gable end, as with the one at Chalkhill Barn (above, see p. 45 for further detail). Cranhill Barn (below) similarly stands in solitary isolation today. Both have been re-roofed as we can see, either with modern concrete tiles or corrugated asbestos cement sheeting, at least protecting the essential fabric of the building.

FINIALS

A not unusual sight, even on quite humble barns throughout the Cotswolds, are a variety of finials – adding a focal point and flourish on a gable end. Most widespread are variations of a simple ball shape. Westwell's Church Farm (above) has these on a square pedestal, together with a curious mid-roof adornment on the ridge. A selection of other shapes can be found on the region's barns in the composite below.

FINIALS

The majority of barns were built on an east–west axis. A novel influence of this phenomenon can be seen on the barn at Hartpury, where a lion faces Wales and a dragon faces England. Some early finials appear perhaps to have had a religious significance, as at Stanway for example; and yet others, though very weathered, still make interesting shapes.

PORCHES

Porches are a major feature of many Cotswold barns. They provided not only protection from the elements for waiting carts to unload their sheaves, but also an extended central floor space for subsequent threshing. The porch at Somerford Keynes (above) has an unusual sundial, while the barley and wheat barns at Cogges (below) provide a variety of gabled and hipped cart entrances with an additional protective canopy over the doorway in one instance.

PORCHES

Particularly attractive is the barn at Church Farm in Barnsley, again with a characteristic protective canopy over the extended porch entrance; the latter could also serve as a temporary cart shed. The tithe barn at Postlip (below) reported to have been used for the wetting and drying of the Winchcombe tobacco crop in the seventeenth century, has a single-porch entrance. The west gable end also has a unique weathered finial, purportedly of Sir Guy de Postlip.

CART ENTRANCES

Inside the cart entrance a square inset hole is often to be found; this was for the grease pot, though some claim it was also the place where a lantern or even a candle was placed to provide light when securing the large double doors from the inside before exiting. Ashleworth (left) is a good example of the large split doors which could be variably opened to provide a controlled draught when winnowing the threshed grain to separate the chaff. One can also see the smaller doors on the opposite side, allowing the now empty carts to exit without turning round.

THRESHING FLOORS

Threshing was an intensive, time-consuming process, normally done in the winter months. A flail was used to separate the ears from the straw before winnowing. During the process low boards or 'thresholds' were sometimes placed across the doorways to prevent the grain from spilling or flying out into the yard – hence the origin of the word, even though the significance of carrying the new wife over the threshold has been lost. These thresholds also had the secondary use of keeping out the farmyard fowl. Many barns had a wooden threshing floor, and below is a rare remaining example at Didmarton.

SCRATCH MARKS, TALLY MARKS AND APOTROPAIC MARKS

It has been suggested that some of the tedium of the threshing process might have been alleviated by keeping a tally of the amounts done by making marks on the jamb-stones of barn doorways. If one studies these entrances closely, many have inscribed graffiti in the form of upright strokes, double overlapping Vs (believed to represent a request to the Virgin Mary to protect the building), as well as a variety of inscribed shapes and circles.

APOTROPAIC CIRCLES
The variety of inscribed circles, frequently with a daisy wheel shape within them, were intended to ward off evil spirits or ghouls.

OTHER INTERPRETATIONS

Two further possibilities have also been
inferred regarding the purpose of these
circles. Joining the intersections in one way
produces either a 30- or 60-degree angle
which could be used for the pitch of a roof.
More convincing is the fact that they can
also be used to provide parallel lines and a
right angle, as shown below for laying out
the floor plan, which has apparently been
found in some barns in other parts of the
country.

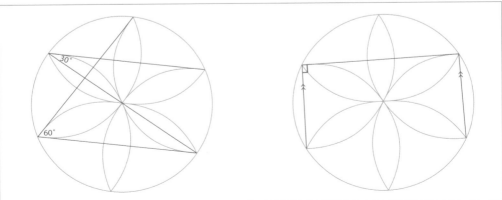

DOORWAYS

Other aspects of craftsmanship on some barns can also give clues as to the original wealth of the owners, essentially acting as a status symbol since they go beyond the merely functional. For example, carved ashlar porticos above a doorway and coursed stonework rather than random rubblestone, as well as mullioned windows, all suggest an earlier prosperous holding.

DOORWAYS

Archways with substantial keystones, rather than simple wooden lintels, also attest to a greater concern with the elegance of the building, as does the fine carved stone arch over the main entrance seen below.

OWL HOLES

High up on the gable end of the barn, the owl hole offers an obvious function: an ingenious provision to actively encourage owls into the barn in order to keep the rodent population down. These holes became more common following a widespread plague of rats in the mid-eighteenth century. Often provided with a convenient perching ledge, they too sometimes took on a somewhat more decorative element.

VENTILATION SLITS

Adequate ventilation is critical both to the fabric of the building, but most importantly to the care of the stored crops. Any residual dampness could rapidly lead to the latter becoming mouldy. Air vents were generally provided in the walls of the barn in the form of narrow chamfered arrow-like slits; a secondary benefit was the letting in of some light when the barn was empty.

VENTILATION

These slits were narrow to keep out the rain and snow, while admitting a flow of air and some light. Apparently unique to the Cotswolds are some ventilation slits which have a diamond-shaped hole above them, giving a 'candle flame'-like appearance. These added features have no known function, and at present I know of just over a dozen or so, spread mainly in the northern half of the region. The square putlog holes (p. 10) were also retained for ventilation.

LOFTED PORCHES

A number of Gloucestershire barns have a lofted area over the cart entrance. At Quenington (above) this appeared to have been used as a granary. The barn also shows the characteristic triangular putlog/ventilation holes which were increasingly common from the eighteenth century. Elsewhere (left) the area was used for general storage as space allowed.

LOFTED SPACES

Some of these lofted areas were accessed by an external flight of steps, some internal; more often it was not overly clear how they were accessed. It would seem from the barn shown to the right that a ladder would most likely have been used, presumably kept some distance away to allow free entrance and exit beneath, as well as for security.

DOVECOTES

An alternative use for many lofted spaces was as a dovecote. A fine example can be seen at Church Farm, Leighterton, built in 1733. (It is also not unusual to see a stone relieving arch above the timber lintel, as shown above.) Access to these dovecotes was generally from the inside, as can be seen below at Furzen Leaze.

DOVECOTES

Simpler versions are often seen, as those at Winterwell (top) and Nympsfield Barn (middle) illustrate. A particularly unusual provision for pigeons can be found at Beverstone (bottom), where some 300 nest holes are seen in an open-ended building. They also illustrate another interesting feature in that the alternate rows of holes curve inwardly to the right or to the left; this was apparently to provide a greater sense of sport for those shooting such birds as they tended always to fly off in the *same* direction if all the holes curved only in one direction.

THE *FERME ORNÉE*

A number of English landlords, unlike their Continental counterparts, often took an active interest in farming matters. One curious outcome of this was the decorative farmstead, often built by a leading architect. In the mid-eighteenth century, Thomas Wright, an architect and astronomer, designed several castellated barns and cow houses on the Badminton estate. The towers and battlements at Castle Barn are essentially a false front, hiding a substantial seven-bay barn behind.

ORNAMENTAL BARNS

Not exactly a folly, the barn at The Old Warren (above) obviously was quite functional and in the Cotswold style despite its castellated and turreted corners. Across the fields from Worcester Lodge, which stands at the end of the three-mile ride entrance to Badminton House, is a further example (below).

IVY LODGE

Cirencester Park provides another illustration of this phenomenon. Ivy Lodge, with its castellated frontage and Gothic windows, has a central square tower, its left gable is merely a screen-wall protecting an orchard, while the opposite gable hides a splendid double-porch barn.

DATING BARNS

Precise dating of many Cotswold barns is not always an easy task, dating by style being the least satisfactory method. Documentary evidence is obviously useful but frequently unavailable for the more humble barns. Saw markings and joint types in the timbers can be helpful, as can dendrochronology in specific circumstances. However, a number of barns have date stones, usually on a gable end – some quite ornate.

MANOR BARN, SOMERFORD KEYNES

A particularly unusual feature on this barn is the date of 1753 which is found on the lower hinge of the final exit door. This appears to be an original piece of ironwork, as it corresponds with the more conventional placing of a date stone on the gable bearing the same date. The internal conversion also shows the relatively rare use of forlock bolts between principal rafters and collars.

CARPENTER'S MARKS

These are a commonly found feature at the junctions of principal rafters, collars and tie beams. The joints would have been measured and cut individually, usually elsewhere, before being raised in place; consequently it was important to retain the correct match. Roman numerals were used in identifying each bay, as straight lines were easier to chisel than curved ones.

THATCHED ROOFS

Thatch was a common sight on many early barns, particularly in the northern Cotswolds, where more corn was grown. It is, however, a rapidly disappearing feature on barns today as a thatched roof requires more regular (and consequently expensive) upkeep than a tiled one.

THATCHING

Thatch sometimes presented a unique problem. Though the roof was able to withstand wind pressure from the outside, if the large barn doors were left open and high winds hit the inside of the roof, then parts of the thatch were likely to lift and even be carried away. A few smaller thatched barns and byres are still to be found.

MORE FIELD BARNS

Field barns continued to be built well into the nineteenth century; many had a variety of animal shelter sheds and additional buildings around an enclosed yard, as with these at Holywe Barn (above) and Winterwell Barn (below).

FIELD BARNS

The vast majority of these now stand abandoned and in splendid isolation, testament to a very different type of farming.

A RARE EXAMPLE STILL IN USE
Though the barn itself is no longer serving any significant functional purpose, the two animal shelters were recently housing a thriving number of pigs.

MODIFICATIONS AND ADAPTATIONS

Barns were rarely, if ever, a static phenomenon. They have always been subject to modifications and changes over time as farming practices and needs changed. At Didmarton (above) we see the addition of stabling and other buildings alongside the original barn. Infill between large porch entrances was also common, saving on further unnecessary building.

ADDITIONS AND MULTIPLE OCCUPANCY
The stabling and animal shelters were obviously an addition to Grange Farm (above). At Ewen (below) we can see that the barn has been adapted to serve a variety of purposes.

54

INCREASING AGRICULTURAL PROSPERITY

The gradually increasing agricultural prosperity has been attributed to the greater power and efficiency of the horse compared with the ox. The replacement of oxen as work beasts also meant an increase in stabling needs. The few aisled barns of the region were one solution; others were simply additions and extensions, as noted; and one or two were very fine purpose-built examples, as seen below, where the bell above the porch was used by the owner to summon his workmen to their tasks.

EXTERNAL STAIRCASES

As smaller barns were adapted for stabling, a lofted area for the storage of hay was often added and this was accessed by external stone steps. Aside from their obvious functional purpose, they frequently provide a very attractive aspect to these buildings, as at Leighterton (below).

FURTHER USES OF STONE STEPS

As well as providing access to the tallat above, the underside of the steps often left a space below which was used as a kennel – and steps of course could be used for mounting a horse.

INCREASING MECHANISATION

The appearance of machinery on farms began in the late eighteenth century with the development of small hand-driven equipment for cutting hay and straw into chaff to reduce wastage by cattle at feeding times, for grinding corn and beans, and for winnowing using a system of sails on radial arms. The preparation of feed for livestock gained ground in the 1830s and 1840s; this often involved the lofting of a section in the barn where chaff cutters and cake breakers were sited. In 1876 Meikle built a winnowing machine, a drum filled with pegs which rubbed and beat the grain from the straw as it rotated.

MOTIVE POWER

Once fixed threshing machines came in, some form of motive power was required to drive them, as well as being needed for machinery used in the preparation of livestock feed. Initially 'horse engines' were used. These were mainly in the open air in the Cotswolds; horses turned a vertical spindle which in turn drove a horizontal shaft (or sometimes a wire cable) running into the barn. In a few cases a purpose-built shelter was constructed adjacent to the barn (as here at Star Farm) to drive the internal machinery via a rotating shaft.

INTERNAL FIXED MACHINERY

The barn was now rapidly losing its traditional function for processing and storing the corn crop and was becoming a processing centre of livestock feed. The remains of belt driven machinery can be seen in these barns at Little Barrington (above) and Oldbury-on-the-Hill (below).

STEAM POWER IN THE COTSWOLDS

With the advent of steam, the entire process continued its revolution. The harvest could await the arrival of the traction engine and steam threshing became a common sight from the 1880s. The machines would trundle from farm to farm – the beginnings of contract farming. An early example was at Hailey (above), and the tradition is being kept alive at Cogges Manor Farm museum (below).

STEAM PLOUGHING

This was achieved by the use of a steel hawser fixed between two steam engines, alternately pulling the plough from one to the other across the field.

FIXED STEAM ENGINES

These were less common and were generally only found on wealthier estates where there was a sufficient demand for their work on a more continuous basis, and an obvious need for a chimney. There was a short-lived interest in feeding cattle on steamed food throughout the winter months. Some use of these engines was also believed to have been made for milling, as at Chesterton farm (above).

THE SARSDEN ESTATE

At one point this estate owned a number of farms in surrounding villages and most of these still have their long since redundant chimneys bearing witness to this earlier period. Some portable steam engines would also need a chimney if they were to drive machinery from within the barn; the majority of these, however, were kept outside the barn with belts to drive a wheel on the end of shafting. Sliding doors, seen below, had also appeared by the 1850s.

MODEL FARMS

The mid-nineteenth century saw the development of a number of so-called model farms, particularly apparent after the various enclosures. These farms were attempts to be more systematic and scientifically organised in the arrangement of the farmyard plan. They were often located around a central barn with a number of cattle sheds, pens and yards, as at Beer Furlong Farm (below). The new cow houses were also ideally suited to the efficient production of manure.

CHASEWOOD FARM

Theories behind model farming often required expensive paraphernalia and buildings which the majority of farmers could not afford. Consequently it was a method which did not last long, as shown in these images of Chasewood Farm when it was taken over in the 1990s.

CHASEWOOD'S RENOVATION

The entire set of farm buildings and yards have, however, undergone a major period of restoration. This has been done virtually entirely to their original design, except for minor modifications, to allow their use as a modern livery. Even the sliding wooden ventilation slats on the buildings' windows have been restored to working operation.

COLLECTOR'S CORNER

Some owners were also collectors and while a small number of barns in the region do have evidence of carved heads on a gable end, none compare with those on Church Farm in Westwell. As well as the usual ball finials there is a very strange mitre-like shape on the ridge, a fine man's head, an animal head, an ammonite and various abstract shapes. These are clearly additions of items too good to simply throw away, reflecting other characteristics of the owner rather than the building per se.

TAYNTON

This too is very obviously the case with a barn in Taynton which has a date stone of 1812 and a clearly inserted medieval lancet window below the conventional pitching hole above (which has fortunately been retained in the building's latest use for domestic accommodation).

EVIDENCE OF INCREASING REDUNDANCY AND DECAY

Sadly, many barns are now not only redundant but also in very poor condition. Once the (expensive) roof has begun to deteriorate, the basic fabric becomes rapidly under threat. This is particularly the case with isolated field barns, which generally have no economic viability whatsoever.

REUSE OF STONE ROOFING
There is a great and understandable temptation to sell the salvageable stone roofing; and even where this has been replaced with modern concrete tiling, little use can be found for the field barn especially.

A FEW, HOWEVER, HAVE CHANGED BUT LITTLE OVER RECENT DECADES

One or two illustrations serve to show how a few still stand relatively untouched. It is doubtful though that they will remain in this state for very much longer, as other pressures will be placed upon them. The majority remain empty or closed up awaiting an unknown future.

SOME MAY BE ACQUIRING A PERIOD CHARM, BUT ...

Redundancy was hastened by a number of factors, some of which we have already seen. In addition there was the repeal of the Corn Laws and the import of cheap grain from the prairies, the increasing reliance on cattle at the expense of arable, and a general agricultural depression in the late nineteenth century. Even buildings kept in good repair are of very limited use, barely accessible to even a moderately sized tractor.

THE MODERN FARMSTEAD
Although the old stone barn may still stand near the farmhouse, even dwarfing it in some instances, they are frequently themselves dominated by the new buildings of today's (often amalgamated) farms with their huge grain stores and dryers, cattle sheds and machinery stores.

CHANGE THOUGH HAS ALREADY COME TO A SUBSTANTIAL NUMBER ...
A large number have already been converted, with varying degrees of sensitivity in terms of their original form, to a variety of uses.

THE CURRENT SCENE

Farm buildings, and especially barns, are under enormous pressure for conversion to alternative uses since so many are redundant and expensive to maintain. It is possible of course to distinguish between absolute loss, through demolition or neglect, and relative loss resulting in loss of character from unsuitable repairs and change. The significance of several of the early surviving barns has been recognised by various charitable trusts, while a number in private hands have been carefully preserved for community use, as at Bourton-on-the-Hill (above) and Postlip (below).

BARNS AS WEDDING VENUES

The use of barns as wedding venues has become quite a widespread phenomenon throughout the Cotswolds. Many have been quite sensitively converted, retaining their essential characteristics of space and much of the original timber work too – even the wooden feed stall and hay rack at Caswell House.

CALCOT

This barn is particularly interesting in that it was a Cistercian barn dating from the early 1300s and has a complete time-line of ownership to the present day where it too is used for wedding venues alongside Calcot Manor Hotel. In 1926 the roof was severely damaged in a winter blizzard and the roof slates were sold, crated up and shipped to America – with the last crate apparently also having a hidden supply of rum for the workers in America who were still 'suffering' the effects of prohibition!

MUSEUMS AND RESTAURANTS

Swalcliffe barn, built between 1400 and 1409, was part of the endowment of New College, Oxford, founded by William of Wykeham, the Bishop of Winchester. It remained in the possession of the College until 1972 and the College archives hold a detailed chronology of its original construction; it also provides a good example of the multi-functional uses and changes which such a medieval barn underwent. It is now used as a museum store for farm machinery and agricultural vehicles. Below is a moderate-sized barn, now the home of a carvery.

WEAVERS AND WORKSHOPS
The Bridal Barn of 1721 at Filkins, so called because it is said to have been used for village wedding feasts in addition to its role as a traditional threshing barn, now houses the Cotswold Woollen Weavers. The associated ox pens, calf pens and outbuildings have been converted into a variety of craft workshops.

IRONGATE FARM, RODMARTON

This provides a typical example of the conversion of redundant outbuildings and shelter sheds for commercial office space. Such conversions do of course rely on the buildings having nearby easy access for vehicles and utilities, which is one reason why many field barns remain in their sorry state.

OX HOUSE TO LIVERY

The Manor at Southrop has recently seen its barns and outbuildings exceptionally well converted for a range of uses, including holiday lettings. The aim has been to maintain the essential integrity of the original buildings: the ox house is now a modern livery, together with some comfortable domestic accommodation.

BARN TO BEANFEAST
The tithe barn's open space has been retained for entertaining and dining, supported by the adjacent well-equipped kitchen for Thyme's cookery courses and food school. The latter also has its own herb garden and produces its own vegetables, and has links to local producers and chefs.

ASHLEY MANOR BARN

The barn above is seen in the process of conversion for domestic use, and below we see the finished state. It has not only retained much of the internal sense of space, but also externally the attached animal shelter sheds have been used to provide a sunny family room overlooking the garden.

CONVERSIONS TO DOMESTIC HOUSING

Despite the strong preference of various agencies for the commercial use of redundant barns, these structures are more often used for domestic housing. If it is simply a conventional modern house you seek, then a barn conversion is not for you. Retaining the essential characteristics of the building is not always easy and certainly not a cheap option. From this external elevation one can be in doubt as to the original purpose of this accommodation at Tarlton.

SETT'S BARN, COATES

Maintaining the sense of space and simplicity are generally the best starting points for a successful conversion. This usually involves the central threshing area as a major source of light, especially if a single space is retained up to the full roof height. Small rooms can often be accommodated at one end, especially when an attached building can be incorporated.

TWO FROM ONE

Even though barns are really only for people who like large open spaces, the large double-porch entrance barn at Somerford Keynes would be excessive for domestic conversion were it not divided into two separate living spaces. Since the roof itself is generally such a dominant feature, sometimes it is only possible to provide an upper galleried area as a practical solution where a living space from ground to ridge is not feasible.

HIGH LIVING
Roof space and timbers can be used to create an area of open living.

LONG LIVING

The essential simplicity of the long barn at Grange Farm has been retained on its eastern elevation during its conversion to three independent living spaces.

RETAINING VENTILATION SLITS ...
Keeping added windows to a minimum can often be achieved by careful utilisation of the ventilation slits, as can be seen here at Shipton Slade Barn before and after its recent conversion.

... AND PUTLOG HOLES

Similarly at Widford, although the putlog holes can realistically only provide interesting features from an internal point of view, the 'puncturing' of the walls has been minimised by the narrow windows which are at least reminiscent of ventilation slits and their symmetry is not obtrusive here. Additional daylight can also be obtained by the use of discreet skylights.

HIGH TUN BARN

The conversion from an integral group of parallel barns of differing length presented a number of spatial challenges here. Evidence suggests the original buildings may have been used as a malthouse with the subterranean water cisterns used as mash pits. Later, the building appears to have been adapted to a large granary, and when model farms and changing methods were influential it is conceivable that the pits could then have been used for liquid manure storage. Today one of these provides a basement swimming pool.

PRICE'S BARN
There is certainly no doubt as to the original occupants of a substantial part of this barn at Southrop.

DURING AND AFTER CONVERSION OF THE RECTORIAL TITHE BARN
All of the essential structural characteristics of this barn have been retained in its conversion.

BIRDS AND BOOKS

The recent transition into a substantial library, with discreet accommodation at either end, has also managed to keep a significant number of the original features, even retaining the nesting holes of the dovecote above the cart entrance.

ACKNOWLEDGEMENTS

While the majority of photographs are from my own collection, I am most grateful for a number of images made available from the following individuals: David Clark, Michael Dallas, Roy Pounder, Roger Sleeman, F. Taylor, Phil Whittaker and Susan Woolley. Thanks also to Peter Keene of 'Thematic Trails' for the production of the map on p. 5; to Adrian Moyes for the digigraph above; to the Corinium Museum, Cirencester; to Country Life; and to Charles & Charles for use of the drawing on p. 10. Grateful thanks are particularly due to Jeremy Lake, June Lewis-Jones, Joan Tucker, David Viner, Lionel Walrond and Alan Watkins for their invaluable suggestions and helpful advice along the way. Especial thanks must obviously go to the many people who gave me access to their buildings, taking me on trust into their homes or around their property, often providing insights which otherwise I would have missed. Thanks to the team at Amberley Publishing for making possible this small reflection of a special part of the countryside and its heritage. Finally, for the continued patience, support and humour from Helen, Sarah and Lucy ... thanks again!